Penelope had many children's stories published in the Lucie Attwell's Annuals. As an artist, she worked on commissions – many for the Armed Forces – and published 'So Many Bridges', telling the events behind these paintings. Recently she wrote and illustrated 'Take Care in Traffic' with Digger Roo for 5–7-year-olds.

She is a Full and Founder Member of the Guild of Aviation Artists.

She lives in Devon.

To my family and friends, who all need a little wubbish in their lives.

Penelope S. Douglas

WHYMES OF WUBBISH
FOR GWOAN-UPS

AUSTIN MACAULEY PUBLISHERS™

LONDON · CAMBRIDGE · NEW YORK · SHARJAH

A CIP catalogue record for this title is available from the British Library.

ISBN 9781528912037 (Paperback)
ISBN 9781528912372 (ePub e-book)

www.austinmacauley.com

First Published (2019)
Austin Macauley Publishers Ltd
25 Canada Square
Canary Wharf
London
E14 5LQ

A

An attractive alligator, Albert he was called,
Was doing aerial aerobatics, when the ancient engine stalled,
Accelerating awkwardly, the aeroplane fell fast,
While Albert, quite appropriately, acknowledged all his past.
With access to an aqueduct, Albert being brave
Allowed the aluminium frame to splash into a wave.
He ambled from the wreckage as the aircraft stayed afloat,
And could adapt, being amphibious, awash without a boat.

An armadillo known as Arthur, asleep upon the turf,
Awaking, grabbed his aqualung and dived into the surf.
Swimming with alacrity through a grey and amber haze
Asked if Albert was alive, for the aircraft was ablaze.
The ambulance awaited them as the animals went ashore.
It was an acceptable adventure, they'd never been in one
before!
Doctors ashen and aghast, appearing very dour,
Said, "It's apparent I'm ashamed to say, they need an
abattoir!"

But the nurses were assertive and astonished at his cry.
"We accuse you of atrocities! You've got no alibi!"
Meanwhile Albert was quite adamant that it simply made
him feel
The approach the nurses had to him, really did appeal!
They were amazed at his anatomy, but appeared to be
confused
Saying he needed an abortion, and Albert was amused!
He applauded all their antics, not an answer did he lack,
And they gave him an aperitif and an aphrodisiac.

Then he became alluring, amorous and free,
Ardently advancing to commit adultery!
With admirable affection, announcing nurses were adored,
As always, ambidextrous, Albert chased them 'round the ward.
Agitated they apologised, but his appetite increased,
So he ate the nurses absently till their "Ahhhs" abruptly ceased.
"They aggravated my aggression," said Albert feeling chaste,
So he and his accomplice left the hospital in haste.

Arthur was articulate in his antediluvian way,
"Eat people by appointment, and average eight a day."
So they announced in an advertisement in an article of taste,
That they'd sort out people's arguments, as fighting was a waste.
Arthur booked appointments in and audited accounts,
Ambitiously accumulating cash in large amounts.
They had an avalanche of customers, the angry and the cross.
Some were acrimonious, and some were at a loss,
With "Au revoir" to losers, Albert admonished to a pulp.
So don't argue or get angry! You'll be swallowed in a gulp!

B

A budgerigar from Bradford was belligerent and bored,
Basically because his flying was bad.
He was brilliant at taking off, but coming down was best!
It was stopping bashed him up and made him mad!
It was bedlam when he landed cos he had such bandy legs,
And bereft of proper balance, banged his beak.
It left him all bewildered, breast bedraggled, black and blue,
With his beak so badly bruised he couldn't speak,
This budgerigar from Bradford.

He bought a brand new boomerang and sat between the
blades,
And buckled up his seat belt for the flight.
But it took him in a circle, and right back where he began,
And bumped him on the branch with all its might!
Now badminton's a game with a shuttlecock that flies,
So he borrowed one and snuggled down inside.
But it bounced him over barricades and barriers galore,
Till he thought he'd broken bones from such a ride,
This budgerigar from Bradford.

He couldn't land from off a bridge, his buoyancy was nil,
He'd be bound to get bronchitis from the wet.
But he'd build a lovely rocket from a battery-powered
broom,
And he'd be the best ballistic missile yet!
So with his biceps bulging, and his little bandy legs,
He launched into the blue sky up above.
And all the Bradford birds turned up to watch him disappear,
With banners wishing, 'All the Best' and 'Love',
To this budgerigar from Bradford.

He landed on a busby of a bugle playing guard
In Buckingham Palace forecourt that same day.
But as usual, lost his balance, and fell into a bassoon,
Which brought havoc to the brass about to play.
The budgerigar was battered but was breathing which was good,
But he'd a bloody beak and badly needed bed.
A footman gave him brandy to banish any pain,
And he began to feel quite chuffed he wasn't dead!
This budgerigar from Bradford.

A bulletin was posted on a Buckingham Palace gate,
Saying, "Budgie's had bicarb and blanket bath.
He's beginning to feel better, had a basin full of broth,
And he's warmed and preened his feathers by the hearth.
He's had blancmange and blackberries from a Buckingham Palace bush,
And is tucked up in his boudoir for the night.
His bandages have been removed, the worst is far behind,
And it's our belief he's going to be all right,
This budgerigar from Bradford."

Now during convalescence, getting better by and by,
The budgerigar was given a balloon.
He made a basket from bamboo that would bend, and hang below,
And it was broadcast he'd be flying again quite soon.
The Beaufort Scale was checked, the barometer said 'Fine'.
He could take off from a balcony that day.
The BBC for 'tele' were allowed inside the gates,
And somebody brought in a big bouquet
For this budgerigar from Bradford.

On the balcony, a footman held the blue balloon quite safe,
And brave budgie in the basket held on tight.
Then he floated down quite beautifully, blown gently by the breeze,
And everyone applauded with delight!

The landing was brilliant! A glass of bubbly was right there,
Also biscuits and a lovely buttered bun.
Now he's floating up to Bradford – have binoculars at hand.
I hope the balloon won't burst! That could be fun
For the budgerigar from Bradford!

C

A coastal caterpillar, Clouded Yellow was his type,
Was confident that music was the best career he'd like.
He was clever on the clarinet, he played it with his feet,
And could convert the best of Chopin to a cool up-tempo
beat.

He was constantly composing, from classical to pop,
And was cantankerous and churlish if called upon to stop.
He'd give some caustic comments that musicians had the
right
To create their own cadenzas in contentment, day or night!

And whilst consuming clover, all crispy from the dew,
With a chilled Chianti wine, then cheese and coffee too,
He calculated carefully he'd form a group or band,
And encourage competition from the insects close at hand.

He advertised conveniently upon the compost heap,
And conducted calm auditions and signed contracts all that
week.
The group was formed with a bumblebee upon the
clavichord:
He'd been a conker champion but complained of getting
bored!

An earwig clashed the cymbals and enjoyed percussion too.
It helped his circulation when his chilblains turned to blue.
A cheerful Cockney cockroach played the cornet with great
style,
And was certain he'd contribute to such culture for a while.

The cricket campanologists rang Canterbury bells,
With a chorus from two centipedes with their counter-tenor yells.
"We'll call ourselves 'The Composts'" was the caterpillar's claim.
"To collaborate for cabaret and concert is our aim!"

Then curiously a crisis came! The Clouded Yellow felt quite ill,
He considered life with caution, and wrote a codicil to his Will.
"My cashmere cardigan's too tight! I'm currently a mess!
I'm convinced I'll be a chrysalis – it's confusing I confess.

I'm confined close to this clematis, it's a complex cure or fate,
My condition's changing chemically. I'm compelled to cling and wait."
They cared and showed compassion as the tears coursed down his cheeks,
And consoled him with a cuddle to cogitate for weeks.

They practised their chromatic scales, cantata, chords and choir,
With cribbage, chess or croquet to pass each waiting hour.
And at a charity performance, I'm certain you should know
That a Clouded Yellow butterfly was the climax of the show.

"A categorical success!" was the comment critics made.
"The 'Composts' were magnificent! How charmingly they played."
The consequence was fame in places close, and quite remote,
With a Clouded Yellow butterfly as a celebrity of note!

D

A delightfully dainty dinosaur had developed a device
For designing deck-chair board games for the beach.
He was determined to develop one that didn't need a dice,
As a three-dimensional puzzle that would teach.

With a date fixed as a deadline for marketing his dream,
He felt despondent and distinctly overwrought.
Unable to decide a decent ending to his scheme,
He was demoralised, disheartened and distraught.

So feeling dehydrated, disagreeable and remote,
He drank a demijohn of delicious damson wine.
And getting decadent, allowed the dregs to dribble down his throat,
Then drunk and dizzy, he deplored his fast decline.

He woke disgracefully dishevelled after a dozen hours in bed,
But felt disturbingly decisive in his views.
He advertised discreetly for a partner it is said,
And disguised it as a crossword in The News.

The first to answer was a dolphin with a devastating brain,
Who dogmatically distributed ideas.
The dinosaur felt defensive and depressed by each refrain,
So dismissed him, dissolving into tears.

A droll and dour dormouse, in a ditty, said he put
Deep devotion both to dominoes and draughts.
But dossed down dozing on a digit of the dinosaur's huge foot,

So was dubiously deployed to other crafts.

But a dynamic little dachshund, with demure and dulcet
voice,
Arrived by car, double declutching through the gears,
And having driven through the drizzle, she deduced the
work her choice,
Displaying the dearest disposition seen for years!

The dinosaur dealt deftly with each detail from the start,
With the dachshund diplomatically distracting!
Saying, "Don't do it that way darling, do it this way dearest
heart,"
For their challenge was deceptively exacting.

The board game was complete, and a difficult deed was
done,
And dictated to a Dictaphone at last.
It was dispatched to meet the deadline of December twenty-
one,
And in demand through all department stores quite fast!

E

An electric eel called Ermintrude from an estuary in Kent,
Was exasperated with her digs and paying excessive rent.
She sold encyclopaedias, an erratic job and tough,
But eventually established she didn't earn enough.
Her talents lay with energy, with current, volts and amps.
She could evaluate economy for using stoves and lamps.
Experienced in emergencies for example, it emerged
She could eject electric shocks that ensured the current surged.
Then in her element as executive with the Electricity Board,
She eagerly expanded into digs she could afford.
But euphoria ended, when with exclamations false and rash,
The chairman exposed the eel of embezzling the cash.
"Your exploits are embarrassing, it's you that we accuse!"
Then Ermintrude was quite enraged and really blew a fuse!
She left them in the dark, unenlightened, in a void,
And emphasised emphatically that she'd be self-employed!

An eider duck called Emily, of European stock,
Had explored the Eastern style of cooking eggs within a wok.
And though a café employee, with exuberance and flair,
She elaborated every dish, to the manager's despair!
Her extravagance endorsed her exotic style and taste,
And with menus so exclusive there was everlasting waste.
When an excursion coach of Eskimos from Exeter arrived,
She thought it most expedient to cook dishes well contrived.
Eight of them had salad, an event which sealed her fate
When an echelon of earwigs expired upon a plate!
The Eskimos' endurance reached a sad and final end.
An epilepsy epidemic sent them 'round the bend!

Emily examined them and offered embrocation,
But they died without emotion – it's no exaggeration!
The manager expelled her, exhausted and annoyed,
And she emphasised emphatically that she'd be self-employed!

An erotic ewe called Emma with ejaculations good,
Gave elocution lessons, exhaling as she should.
Running errands for an Embassy, the Egyptian one I'm told,
Her expanding ego and exhilaration made her bold.
She was enthralled with all the elegance, and the men there gave her scope,
And enchanting one such envoy she enticed him to elope!
Emma said in error, "How exquisite! We're engaged!"
But he became excited and explained he was enraged!
She entwined her feet around him and whispered in his ear,
"You can't eradicate my love. I'll educate you dear!"
He told her she had eavesdropped and endangered every plot.
"It's the equivalent of espionage! I don't envy you a lot!
In this envelope is evidence – an enlargement is enclosed!"
Then Emma felt entranced to think at last she'd been exposed!
He chased her as she made escape, which she thoroughly enjoyed,
And she emphasised emphatically that she'd be self-employed!

So the electric eel and eider duck and erotic ewe have gone
As a backing group together, to work with Elton John.
As extroverts, exhibiting such talents that these four
Are engrossed in entertaining in England, on tour.
They envisage wealth and fame, with ease they work throughout the nights,
Ermintrude is quite switched on, engineering disco lights.
She joins Emily and Emma in exclusive cabaret,
And they exert themselves and sing in an extraordinary way.
Emma flutters eyelashes that capture every heart,

Embellishing herself in ermine stole to do her part.
They're exploding into stardom, and that they can't avoid,
And emphasise emphatically it's great being self-employed!

F

On Friday, two fat frogs
Favoured wooden clogs
As a foreign form of boat,
For they found that they would float.
And frequently their task,
With fruit and food and flask,
Was to feast 'till they were full –
And give the oars a pull.
Freda liked fried fish,
It formed her favourite dish.
Fred liked frozen food.
It put him in the mood
To function on his flute,
While Freda played the lute.
The forecast was force five
Which with finesse they could survive.
But it freshened and it filled,
And they figured they'd be killed.
Then Fred began to freeze
In the fresh and fickle breeze.
He was frozen to the bone,
And was fossilised in foam.
Freda, frightened she might fail
In the foul and filthy gale,
Felt she'd formulate a flame
For her far from flimsy frame,
And feigned fictitious heat
To her fat and flabby feet.
She feared her clog would sink,
When she hit fluorescent pink!
It was flamingos in a trance,

Doing a fierce flamenco dance!
In forty fathoms they were tough,
Treading water in their fluff,
But with a fascinating pounce,
From a flourish and a flounce,
One swallowed Freda in a flash,
Which was foolish and so rash!
For their fundamental fuel
Is not froggies as a rule,
And being fastidious in taste,
Eating Freda was a waste.
But they flew off from the sea
In formation to Fiji.
But Freda frolicked down inside,
Feeling frivolous from the ride!
She formed a fricassee of froth!
(The frenzied bird began to cough)
Her formula had sense
For causing frantic flatulence!
The bird was furious, and did fret
Like a feathered flageolet,
And was sick, which was a bore
In a flood upon the floor.
Out flopped Freda, fine and free,
Far from being a fatality!
Fortunes of frogs can fluctuate.
It's fantastic the way they can migrate!

G

A gander in galoshes was gambolling in a gale,
Munching garibaldi biscuits to prevent him feeling frail.

He'd gorged himself on garlic in a gastronomic feast,
And had gargled in his gizzard 'till the stench of it had
ceased.

He'd gathered wives galore, whilst ignoring Gretna Green,
And a more gorgeous glut of goosey girls never had been
seen!

It was grand to be at home with geraniums in bloom,
And it was great to greet each day and watch the sun burst
through the gloom.

He could grub around the gloaming with its dewdrop
gleaming threads,
While spiders gossiped gravely on their graceful gossamer
webs.

He was gawky in galoshes but danced a gay and lively gig,
Then giddy, giggled, watched by a gesticulating pig!

The pig threw down the gauntlet with a gregarious merry
grin,
For some guttural verbal sparring, and as a gourmet she'd
begin…

"They'll make a gravy from your giblets," she gloated with
such glee,
"And garnish you with groundsel, and that I'll guarantee!

The guillotine will make you gulp!" she grunted in delight.
"They'll grill your legs, they'll be the most gelatinous thing
in sight!"

The gander started a gavotte, eyes gleaming he replied,
"They'll blow you up with gelignite which will lead to
genocide!

They'll behead you for a gargoyle and serve you up as pork,
Or you'll end up as a gammon and be guzzled with a fork!"

They always grappled verbally on their goals and shared
their strife.
Let us grant good friends and neighbours, a long and healthy
life!

H

Hannah Herring from the Hebrides, a hypochondriac,
To Harley Street and hospital she'd been,
But she hadn't had hysteria nor a haemoglobin lack,
And neither haemorrhage nor hernia could be seen.

So with heart and hearing perfect, she harangued the
haughty nurse
Who didn't hesitate to say her health was fine,
And prescribed a happy holiday as she didn't need a hearse,
With hints of Honiton or Hampshire, or the Rhine.

Hannah hurried home to Hampstead, as only herrings can,
And had some honeycomb and ham to help her throat.
She'd holiday with friends, and they'd meet to make their
plan
For somewhere handy and not horribly remote.

She didn't fancy Heidelberg, nor a Himalayan hike,
Nor Hawaii, nor a hotel near a port.
She was very hypercritical, and to be honest, what she'd like
Would be to visit the historic Hampton Court.

Henrietta Halibut, a friend that Hannah 'phoned,
Had hiccups and a heavy dose of 'flu.
She looked hideous when sneezing, and with engagements
postponed,
Just howled into her handkerchief anew.

"Take a healing herbal drink," said Hannah on the line,
"Then hypnotise yourself in restful pose.
You sound hoarse and very husky, and with sleep you'll
soon be fine,
And it's hereditary to hibernate and doze."

Now Harriet, a Haddock, a humble humorous fish,
Went hurtling through her horoscope each day.
To head away from hazards that could haunt her was her
wish,
In case a harpoon or a fishhook came her way.

Her horticultural habit was for growing hybrid flowers,
With hydrangeas and hyacinths sublime,
And hollyhocks and harebells, the hobby took her hours
And her handicap was often lack of time.

But she had hallucinations that a hawk had killed her plants,
And was horrified and hurt at such a scene.
Then Hannah said a holiday from hardship would enhance,
And that Hampton Court was where she'd never been.

So Harriet and Hannah, and Henrietta too,
Packed a haversack, and nothing did they lack,
And in harmony, they hijacked a hippo from the zoo,
Harnessing a howdah to its back.

"We'll have no hanky-panky, then we'll handle you with
care,"
Said Hannah to the hippopotamus hide.
"Now hasten off to Hampton Court! Your bulk will soon be
there.
First to Hyde Park, then to Holland Park we'll ride."

But after just an hour the hippo hobbled to a stop,
Humiliated by his tender hooves.
So at a haberdasher, and a store where they could shop,
They hired some hobnail boots and pretty shoes.

They bought a huge harmonica, a harpsichord and horn,
And heaved and hauled them up to howdah height.
"We'll play some tunes from Haydn and we'll herald in the dawn,"
But soon the hippo hero halted for the night.

So the herring and haddock and the halibut with a smile,
Hung their hammock from some handsome hawthorn trees,
And lay down head to tail, horizontal for a while,
Rocked to sleep by a haphazard sort of breeze.

From a handy house, the hippo found a hose, and took a sip,
Being hampered by hot weather and the heat.
He made a lovely pool of water and a hollow for his hip,
And took his heavy weight from off his feet.

At Hampton Court next day, all was havoc and a haze,
For it happened Henry VIII was on the throne.
"We've all gone back in history!" gasped Hannah in a daze.
"I feel harassed and I want to be alone!

I hate King Henry VIII, for he'll harm us come what may!
This isn't funny! Not hilarious! Not a laugh!
A helicopter would hoist us up, high above the fray,
But we'll end life in a hay box in the hearth!"

"Come hither!" said King Henry. "I quite fancy having fish!
They'll make a very hearty second course.
If they haven't got a hallmark, have them served upon a dish
With some hollandaise – a very special sauce!

I want a hearty meal, as I'm hungry and must sup,
So behead those fish and halve them down their spine.
They'll make a huge and tasty helping. Now hurry! Serve them up!
And pray take note that all three fish are mine!"

So a hard and harrowing ending to the hapless fishes three,
Of halibut and haddock, herring too.
But the hippo being honest, said he hankered to be free,
And hitch-hiked home via Hammersmith to the zoo!

I

An illegitimate ibex in his Icelandic igloo home,
Though indigenous to ice and snow and cold,
Was not impervious to leaving, and whilst ironing, idle thoughts
Made him impetuous, illogical and bold.

Inexperience did not impair his indomitable mind,
Imagination proved innocuous you see.
And as an intrepid traveller, he intended going far,
So packed his sledge quite instantaneously.

Instrumentally equipped, he played on his trombone
An impromptu intermezzo loud and clear.
Such an inexplicable noise at an interception in his path,
Made an iguana instantly appear!

"That noise is irresistible, I'm really most impressed!
You've inspired me on this inauspicious day.
My fellow actor's indisposed with inflammation in his eye,
So I implore you, please perform in Ibsen's play."

Their effort was impeccable and indelible to watch.
Indeed the impact of it couldn't be ignored.
But the audience showed ingratitude and indignation too.
They were illiterate and ignorant and bored!

Inclement weather interrupted with lightning overhead,
And it came like an incendiary in the night.
It ignited and incinerated props! The wooden stage
Glowed indigo with incandescent light.

The ibex indulged in improvising all his words,
But inaudible, he gave up with a choke.
Inarticulate and inhaling, the iguana tried to talk,
But they were incommunicado through the smoke!

The ibex was intact and the iguana too,
They had neither died intestate nor been hurt.
With insurance irredeemable, impulsively they left,
Inseparable, and inexplicably pert!

They insist they're with Intelligence, based on the Isle of
Wight,
So with international intrigue they're involved.
They investigate by interview, introductions from abroad,
And imperturbably, each incident is solved!

They're incredibly inconspicuous, indispensable as well,
Working incognito and disguised,
Inoffensively innocuously mingling with a crowd,
Selling items of insecticide for flies!

So when insects are a nuisance, avoid them if you can,
Information on your lifestyle is being sought.
Iguana and ibex will check your bank account at once,
And you wouldn't wish to face those two in court!

J

Josephine was a jellyfish with a jovial, jaunty air,
And although she had a nasty sting, using it was rare.

She was jogging from a jumble sale, and hadn't journeyed
far,
Having bought japonica jam in a jonquil coloured jar.

She pretended to be jocular though feeling far from brave,
When a judo loving lobster jumped upon her from a cave.

She thought, "I'll sing Jerusalem and show I do not care!
I'm Josephine the jellyfish with a jovial, jaunty air!"

He frightened her and got her wedged against a jagged rock,
And though she had the jimjams, she said, "See you in the
dock!"

The case came up in court – it was January the third,
And the lobster used such jargon he was lucky to be heard!

The journalists were jotting down each good judicial point,
While the lobster jerked his muscles and flexed each and
every joint!

"I'm a jinx on every jellyfish and want to cause them pain.
I meant to jostle her and threaten, and pinch her jugular vein.

I'd make a julienne of her! She'd be a juicy broth!"
But the jury didn't like the joke or his horrid, wheezing
cough.

He juggled with his evidence and jabbered on at length,
While the judge drank jugs of orange juice, and murmured,
"Give me strength!"

Though Josephine felt jittery at his jesting, jaundiced guile,
She jettisoned each ugly thought, and sat there with a smile.

"You jabbed me with a jemmy and you nearly smashed my
jaw!
It hit me like a javelin, and you broke the ocean law!"

It wasn't just his jacket or his scruffy jeans and shirt.
It was his jeering, jealous nature, and he'd clearly meant to
hurt!

The jury thought him juvenile, and justice must be done.
With joy the case was over, and the jellyfish had won!

The judge was jubilant and thankful, and gave a happy sigh.
"We'll hold a jolly jamboree in June or in July.

We'll combine it with the jubilee of my job of being a
judge!"
And then he winked at Josephine and gave her quite a
nudge!

The day came, and the jellyfish enhanced her pretty face
With some salmon coloured lipstick, and a shawl of jet-
black lace.

And opening her jewel box of jaconet and shell,
In a jiffy picked some jewellery that showed her beauty well.

She chose a coral necklace, with jasper, pearl and jade,
And put rings on every tendril 'till a jangling noise was
made.

The judge and jellyfish joined up, and danced a merry jig.
Then he whispered to her gently, "I look young without my wig!

Life is just a jungle! You must joust with it I'm told!"
Then he lovingly gave Josephine a Jacobus of gold.

They jived and did the jitterbug – which was currently the rage,
While the band played jazzy music, juxtaposed upon a stage.

And if you get in a jam, don't just quit, and don't despair.
Be like Josephine the jellyfish with a jovial, jaunty air!

K

Kleptomania in my kangaroo is difficult to stop!
She slips things in her pouch in just a trice.
If I kindly ask to search her, she takes off at the hop.
I don't think kangaroos are very nice!
Even stuffed with kapok!

Now kindergarten training would be just the very thing,
But she pinched the toys and knick-knacks off the kids.
So I kept her in the kitchen, where I'd jars to keep things in,
But I knew her furry paws could undo lids!
Paws stuffed with kapok!

As a kid I learnt to knit, so I made a khaki scarf,
And knotted it around her furry throat.
She borrowed my kimono, and her antics made me laugh!
Beneath it she'd got knickers, kilt and coat!
And a body stuffed with kapok!

She got teased by other children, but she'd never sulk or
pout,
And if occupied, perhaps she wouldn't steal.
But she got bruised around the kidneys, and was kicked and
knocked about.
I put kaolin on her foot to help it heal.
A foot stuffed with kapok!

I'd kindle other interests, take her camping down in Kent,
So filled a knapsack with the kit we'd need to take
But she kidnapped all the car keys, so I couldn't pack the
tent,
And I knew that it was all a big mistake,

To take my kangaroo, stuffed with kapok!

I read her Keats and Kipling, and she listened with such
poise!
I told of kittiwakes, and kestrels and their kill.
A kaleidoscope and kayak are her very latest toys,
And a kite she's keen on flying from the hill,
With paws stuffed with kapok!

I thought a different diet might kerb her thieving kink,
Like kedgeree and kippers, and kebabs,
But she still stole all the ketchup and created quite a stink
When I said my keepsakes weren't just up for grabs,
From arms stuffed with kapok!

"Oh go home to your kith and kin, koalas and all,
And join the laughing kookaburra bird!"
But she climbed upon my knee, snuggled close beneath my
chin,
Gave me kisses, and said she hadn't heard!
Ears stuffed with kapok!

So she's still a kleptomaniac, and I cannot make her see,
For she keeps on getting 'round me with her charms!
I put the kettle on, and we have a cup of tea,
Then kneeling down, I take her in my arms.
A heart stuffed with kapok? Oh no!

L

Laura, a llama, was lamenting to herself,
Of late she'd got so lazy, limp and frail.
But tests from the laboratory gave the verdict on her health.
She'd got leukaemia, and that's why she was pale.

The doctor lingered long on death, and offered her a port,
Saying she'd languish fast 'till life was at an end.
She was livid and at loggerheads with the lesson that he
taught,
Which she logically refused to comprehend.

She'd laboured long and hard, working early, working late
Through a labyrinth of problems and of strife.
So she'd liquidate her firm, get her ledgers up to date,
And make the most of leisure, love and life.

She felt it wasn't lunacy to take a lengthy cruise,
As she longed to look at London and the Thames.
Go by lugger or by liner? It was difficult to choose.
"Now listen! Do not linger!" said her friends.

She had very little money, but was loathe to just give in.
She'd have to get a loan or she'd be stuck.
But she got left a legacy of an uncle's lottery win,
So was legitimately loaded, which was luck!

She drank over half a litre of liquorice liqueur,
To lubricate herself to leave Peru,
Lifting labelled luggage up the gangway from the shore
And arrived quite sloshed on board the QE2!

Her language was obscene, and she sometimes gave a sigh,
She was loquacious, loud and lively, and quite drunk!
But in a lucid moment sang a lilting lullaby
That led to languidly collapsing on her bunk!

She gave up drinking liquor – just a lager now and then,
Writing letters on her cruise, and playing lacrosse,
And at last arrived in London where she went to find Big
Ben,
And for once, for words was totally at a loss!

You can locate her down in Lambeth in a long-lease loft, it's
said,
With a lobby full of landscapes, quite a place!
The carpets in her lounge are in loganberry red,
With lamps of lilac and lobelia coloured lace.

Her leukaemia has gone, she's a legend more and more,
For she's a liberated llama, and in love!
She's giving language lessons, over liquorice liqueur,
And says her gifts are sent her from above!

M

A maggot from Mauritius with a Mona Lisa smile,
Manufactured millinery of a most bewitching style.
Some of them were mackintosh to wear in a monsoon,
With muff or mittens that were monogrammed, and proved
to be a boon.
Some were mustard coloured with mink or monkey trim,
Or had mock marigolds or mulberries arranged around the
brim.
Many soft materials had ribbons made to match,
And her midnight black mantillas were a memorable catch!
The prettiest hats were muslin, in magenta, mauve and pink,
With marvellous feather edging either straight or with a
kink.
She marketed her merchandise with maturity and flair,
And miraculously soon became a multi-millionaire!
But a miserable mishap became a major threat!
It wasn't measles or malaria that was causing her to fret.
Melancholia set in, because she'd got the mumps,
And her mandibles were moulded between two massive
lumps!
Mortified, morale was low, her mysterious smile had fled!
With many muscles aching she took to medicine and bed,
With mulligatawny soup, and molasses in her milk.
It was a mistake for mumps to happen to a maggot of her ilk!
Feeling morbid, she imagined dying like Marie Antoinette,
When to end up in a mortuary would be mere etiquette!
Of such misconceived ideas she was mercifully free
When she munched a marmite muffin, and drank a mug of
tea.
Then on a Monday morning she moved to Paris in late
March,

36

Under no misapprehension she'd miss majestic Marble
Arch.
Museum meditation gave her magic, mental peace,
Enjoying the medium used by Monet, by Manet and Matisse.
She was mesmerised by Mahler, thought the mandolin was
cute,
And loved the music that was Mozart's and his moving
Magic Flute.
She meandered through Montmartre, and the Moulin Rouge
was good,
And with metabolism perfect she'd been as mobile as she
could.
The maggot moved to London, leaving Paris at mid-day,
Suntanned to mahogany in the merry month of May.
She met a maladjusted mollusc who had great magnetic
charm,
In a monetary muddle that would do his mortgage harm.
He mauled her on a mattress, this maternal maggot maid,
She mumbled into his moustache, "Don't molest me! I'm
afraid!"
Moistening her lips she said she felt misunderstood!
Merging money in a marriage, would do no mutual good.
"It would be a misalliance and a sheer monstrosity!
I'll forgive you your misconduct – it's my mission to be
free!"
The mollusc moped and muttered, myopic, which was vile,
And must have been misled by the mischief in her smile!
Now she's a mannequin and modelling hats, in a marquee,
With many medals from our Monarch which includes the
M.B.E.!
Visit 'Millinery of Mayfair', it's been there quite a while,
And meet the maggot from Mauritius with the Mona Lisa
smile!

N

Neville Newt was playing a nocturne in a concert in New York,
With numerous interruptions for applause.
He was not a novice at the piano, and played the notes with style,
And the necessary nimbleness of paws.

He'd cross the North Atlantic, not a doubt was in his mind.
He'd design a boat, and soon be under way.
Neither nagging nor persuasion could nudge aside his plan.
Now or never, was his feeling, come what may!

Swimming should, of course you'd think, be second nature to a newt,
But not Neville! He'd been nurtured other ways.
His parents had been negligent, neglecting such a skill,
And so normal breaststroke left him in a daze!

His craft was made of ginger nuts, with a nine-inch nail as mast,
A nasturtium flower was a pretty spinnaker sail.
Hollow nutmegs added buoyancy from any noxious seas,
And were held with nylon thread to form a rail.

Although he couldn't swim, he was nautical at heart,
And navigated from the narrow port.
Someone notified the Press, and they noisily took notes
To put Neville in the news just as they ought.

Being November it was foggy, but he steered course nor-
nor-east,
Negotiating every trough and wave.
But noticing at noon one day, the wind was blowing up,
He was nervous, and no longer feeling brave.

He felt numb and had a notion that Neptune was at hand.
The nape of his neck felt colder than a grave.
He had a nuisance of a nightmare of some nuns in Notre
Dame
Singing the Nunc Dimittis in the nave.

But if nothing else, Neville was not negative at all.
He'd learnt to grasp the nettle that was life.
He'd throw non essentials overboard, keep only what he'd
need,
Enjoying the novelty of such nocturnal strife.

He nosed the ginger nut into the nucleus of the storm,
Then nodding, had a nap before some food,
Seeking nourishment, he nibbled at some nougat on his
bunk,
And nullified his nasty, nervy mood.

Whilst netting fish for dinner was a noose to nab them with,
A nymph from nether regions came on board.
Not naked in the nude, but in a nighty spun from silk,
And with naughty smile, was instantly adored!

She seemed to come from nowhere, was noble, neat and
trim,
And nestled closely to him on the deck.
He narrated his adventures, nattering non-stop,
While she nuzzled him and nibbled at his neck!

He thought he'd tie the nuptial knot with this new and lovely
bride,
But of necessity, from wind was forced to tack,

And arriving near the Needles, to the water she returned,
And he'd lost his precious nymphomaniac!
He searched and called quite needlessly, for naught was
there to find.
He felt nostalgic for the neon lights of home.
So he hitched a ride on a nightingale that was heading for its
nest,
Being nonchalant – he'd no more wish to roam.

His nasal sense and nostrils loved the smell of Norfolk mud,
Where narcissus bloomed 'neath vast and native skies.
Based on life, he wrote a novel, and he used a non de plume,
And for literature, he won the Nobel Prize!

O

Oswald was an ostrich as I'm sure you will have heard,
And with his ochre colouring, a quite outstanding bird.
He worked in an observatory, a most obnoxious task,
And when he ordered overtime, they said he shouldn't ask!
He'd often sit up half the night, observing all the stars,
But overslept one evening, oblivious to Mars.
Orion was in orbit, but Venus was obscured,
And he offered an opinion that frankly he was bored,
And so he left!

Ophelia was an Osprey, so pretty, young and gay,
Occupied in office work, and not outdoors all day,
Selling oblong ottomans and oval chairs in oak,
And ornaments and ovens 'till her voice became a croak!
Her oesophagus was swollen and her optimism gone!
"I'm obsolete!" she wailed, "And it's gone on far too long!"
So she became obstreperous, and it'll come as no surprise
They said she was outrageous when she asked them for a
rise!
And so she left!

Obediah was an owl, and orphaned long ago,
An outspoken sort of fellow with a past you shouldn't know!
So he became a lawyer, often under oath in court,
Giving many an oration, and saying more than he ought!
He'd should out loudly, "I object!" when each offence
occurred.
"Objection overruled!" they said, "Now not another word!
You're obstructing the proceedings! You're officious! Be
obscure!

41

We'll have you ordered out of court if you interrupt once
more!"
And so he left!

Our trio met in Oxford at one o'clock next day,
To overcome the obstacles of being without pay.
They observed that they could often sing in octaves high and
low,
From oriental music to the Oklahoma show.
They auditioned for an opera, Ortello was the name,
And with orchestra and organ, obtained immediate fame!
An overture from Offenbach got outbursts of applause!
People wanted autographs and hammered at the doors!
So should they leave?

Many an ovation brought people to their feet,
And orchids were presented, and even things to eat!
They lived on onion omelettes and olives soaked in brine,
And octopus and oysters, and oranges in wine.
Many opportunities were offered from abroad,
And soon they had the OBE and were knighted with the
sword.
So now they're off to Ottawa, to Oslo and Milan,
But they'll opt for Covent Garden, which is their future plan,
And so they left!

P

A precocious, pretty penguin, released from prison on parole,
Hadn't planned to be pernicious as a thief.
It was a passion for collecting 5P pieces that she stole,
And pick pocketing led to punishment and grief!

So Prunella, on probation gave a profound and grateful sigh.
But was perplexed to know what pastime to pursue.
Making pastry on her porch for a plaice and pilchard pie,
She philanthropically decided what to do.

Painting pictures and patterns onto porcelain in haste,
Portraying portraits of a Post-impressionist style.
With perspective rather poor she smashed the plates – perhaps a waste,
So gave up palette, paints and pastels for a while.

Punctiliously, she was pleased to try a parachute instead,
But pondered, being a psychopath, to try.
If she perished in a pulp she'd need a pathologist if dead,
And felt painfully pessimistic when up high!

And though she pleaded quite politely with the pilot of the plane,
She was paralysed with panic, which seemed silly.
But she plunged with great panache, penetrating cloud and rain,
With a panoramic view of Piccadilly!

Like professional musicians she'd perform in public for a change,
So joined the Philharmonic Orchestra too,
With the Prince of Wales as patron: she knew their phrasing and their range,
Playing Prokofiev's Piano Concerto number two.

But Prunella had yet to find the perfect job to thrill,
And must not pilfer purses in the street.
She could neither pole a punt, nor work a pneumatic drill,
Nor be a peddler selling palatable treats.

She entered the pentathlon – of a medal she'd be proud,
But the pistol shot made people's pulses race!
It peppered all the pellets in the proximity of the crowd,
Which left them prostrate, puce and purple in the face!

Competing hard at ping-pong, left her in the dumps,
But she danced at the Palladium and looked sweet,
Pirouetting purposefully in pale pink satin pumps,
Then needed physiotherapy for her feet!

Then suddenly, her problem solved, she promised that she'd won,
And being particularly patient had been right.
She was paddling in a pool on the pavement in the sun,
And became a 'Puddle Jumper' overnight!

There were paragraphs of publicity in the papers all next day.
She was profoundly photogenic too you see.
She puddle jumped with a parasol, adding propulsion in its way,
And was promoted for a programme on TV!

Q

Quintin was a quadruped
A fox with bushy tail.
In Queen's at Cambridge he'd a place,
And felt he couldn't fail.

He was quaint but he was lazy,
And he quibbled with the staff.
He would not quell his idleness,
And took the easy path.

A quarter of his lectures
Were on quarries full of quartz.
But when faced with an exam
The fox was really out of sorts!

The questionnaire was worded
Like a quiz, and made him quake!
He argued with examiners
Which was a stupid bad mistake.

Quintin said, "These questions
Do not take the usual form.
I think that I'd be better off
If hunting with the Quorn!

I'll quit on this exam,
And throw quill and quire away!
If I quarrel with authority
I'm querulous to-day!

I'll put myself in quarantine,
And order quail and mince,
And though it makes me queasy,
I'll finish with a quince.

I'll have it served in bed,
And pretend I'm feeling queer.
And as long as no one tells the 'quack',
I'll quench my thirst with beer!"

In the quietness of his room,
As he sat beneath his quilt,
He queried his behaviour
'Till quivering with guilt.

"I've done quantities of work,
And I'm not a stupid nit!
I'll struggle from this quagmire,
And I'll start by getting fit!

I know a healthy body
Means a quick and healthy mind.
I'll quash each quest or rumour
That I'm lagging far behind!

I'll go to the quadrangle
And play quoits upon the grass.
I'll still have time to qualify
If I only get a Pass!"

He stretched his lungs on quavers,
And sang in a quartet.
And his qualities were mentioned
In the Quarterly Gazette.

His quandary was over,
No more qualms for an exam,
For he'd take his ancient boat

And get fit upon the Cam!

He couldn't quant his Quinquereme,
It's difficult with paws,
So with quintuplet and quorum
He joined them at the oars.

After supper in the evening
He danced in a quadrille.
His fitness helped his written work,
And learning was a thrill!

He qualified quite easily
With a First, just as he ought,
And left there as a Cambridge Blue
In music, dance and sport!

R

Rosie was a rhino who could not pronounce her 'R's,
She got ridiculed if reading out aloud.
She never once rebuked her friends, it didn't rankle her at all!
"I'm weady to see the funny side," she vowed.

She was very often ravenous, and it was rhubarb she adored.
The rascal could eat it by the hour!
Though reluctant to admit this, she reminded all her friends,
"It's not widiculous! I weally like it sour!"

But the rhino was recalcitrant, repugnant, not her best.
They tried Welch rarebit and rich rice which had been fried.
"Now if I was a waven, wook or wobin on her nest,
I could wegurgitate the whubarb from inside!"

So Rosie wanting rhubarb felt rebellious and rash,
And wished to ravage with a razor, all in reach!
With a revolver and a rifle, she ranted and she raved,
"I'll pay a weal weward or wansome" was her speech.

A randy rodent felt romantic, his name was Rodney I recall,
And ratifying his love, he pressed his suit.
Radiant, he rambled on, but this was her response,
"It's a whetowical sort of question! Where's my fwuit?"

She reproached herself quite rigorously for not being so rotund,
For remember she was getting rather thin.
Remorsefully reminding them she was losing her reserve,
"You'll wecognise wigormortis setting in!"

She rejected food like raisins, radishes or a roast,
"I'll be a wecluse and welic of my day!
Did Wossini wight a Wecuiem?" she weepingly inquired.
"I'm wepulsive and wevolting! Go away!"

Someone recommended rhubarb! The season had returned,
And with relief she ate, no longer feeling faint.
"I'm the wecipient of some whubarb!" she rapturously said.
"I can weveal that I can eat without westwaint!"

She's revived and quite redeemed, rampant, not reformed,
Robust and rowdy, and rosie cheeked I found.
"There's been a wevolution! I've done wesearch!" she could relate,
"I've bought a fweezer, so it's whubarb all year wound!"

S

A scorpion with a stammer in a southern Shetland Isle,
Was so scared of life, so sensitive and shy.
He was significantly silent, sporadic sentences his style,
Saying, "I'm s-s-stricken with a st-st-stammer, and that's w-w-why!"

He was shrewd enough to summarise speech therapy should help,
So in September he would steadfastly go south.
He'd leave the sheep and Shetland sweaters, the sporrans and the kelp.
Or shamefully forever shut his mouth!

So he sailed south to the mainland – the swell he couldn't watch.
He was seasick, soused and sodden from the spray.
He sampled salmon sandwiches, some shortbread and some Scotch,
But was sorry and saliferous all day.

He'd see the winter sports in a solitary spot,
Seeking silence, for he could scarcely speak.
But the standard of the slalom simply wasn't all that hot,
He thought sardonically the skiing was somewhat weak!

He summoned all his courage and asked the sponsors, "C-c-can I s-s-ski?"
As shaking, he sucked sherbet through a straw.
He slid down the slopes so sportively, side-slipping was the key,
Slashing several splendid seconds off the score!

In his seersucker shirt, snow shoes and sheepskin coat,
He'd climb Snowdonia and find solitude once more.
Surveying his footsteps in the sleet, he felt serious and remote,
In these surroundings he stood still, no longer sure.

His survival now was slender, he dug a shelter near some rocks,
Made a shallow scrape, staggering under stress.
He couldn't shout with such a stutter, so to a stick secured his socks,
And semaphored the signal, 'S.O.S'.

He was salvaged, semi-conscious, by the S.A.S. of course,
And they skilfully set up a saline drip.
They shared a brew, and their spaghetti in a savoury, spicy sauce,
After sewing several stitches in his lip.

Saying, "T-t-thank y-y-you!" to the soldiers, he hired a supersonic bike,
And our scorpion on his scooter squealed with fun!
And strapping up his stomach, said, "I'll d-d-do some s-s-scrambling which I l-l-like,"
And was showered with champagne when he won!

He played soccer in a stadium with shrieking from the stands,
As he sprinted up the field to score the goals.
He was a star and a sensation and was swamped by screaming fans
Who shredded all his clothing into holes!

At Sheffield he played snooker, struck each ball supremely well,
His success showed with surprise upon his face.
He surreptitiously surmounted all his nerves as he could tell,
And beat Steve Davis into second place!

The scorpion sniffed some snuff in seclusion far away,
And sat in shafts of sunlight in a glade.
He still felt soothed by being solo, could keep social life at bay,
And stared into the secrets of the shade.

He gave a supercilious sneer at the stutter in his voice.
"I'm a great s-s-success at sp-sp-sport, of th-th-that I'm s-s-sure!"
With solemnity he saw that life's solution was his choice.
"N-n-now my st-st-stammer doesn't m-m-matter any m-m-more!"

How stimulating life can be, so sparkling and great,
Or it struggles by as sluggish as a snail.
When things are going superbly and in stupendous state,
Fate often has a sting within the tail!

T

A tadpole from Tasmania was famous throughout town
For trampolining, tight-rope acts, and balance of renown.
Her twists and turns were famous, to watch her was a treat.
Her twirls were quite tremendous with her wonderful technique.
But on Tuesday in a tea house, the tight-rope broke in three,
And she tumbled with a thud on to the people taking tea!
She tore herself quite terribly, and blood flowed far and wide,
While they talked to her so tenderly and tried to stem the tide.
Her trembling little torso, 'twas not a pretty sight,
And where her tail began, they put a tourniquet too tight.
They trussed her in a tablecloth and telephoned the news,
And doctors came on tricycles and arrived in ones and twos.
They thought how they should treat her in the twilight of her day,
But the tourniquet had tightened and her tail broke clean away!
It slithered from her body, and the tense and worried host
Didn't realise what had happened and he ate it on his toast!
The doctors had a tête-à-tête, and clearly they were tense.
"We must replace her tail although the problem is immense!
We'll have to try a transplant – it's a tricky sort of thing
For the trouble with a tadpole is to know where to begin!
I think a pair of trousers ought to help her dainty tread,
In towelling or taffeta, in terracotta red."
"We'll stick them on with treacle," said a doctor through his teeth,
"And tie them on if necessary with thread from underneath."
The tributes to her talent came in trebles thick and fast,

And the Telegraph typed out an obituary to her past.
The doctors tacked the trousers on, with tweezers and with twine,
And although her temperature was high, they felt she would be fine.
She convalesced with tonic and a trip to Tenerife,
And returned to trampolining, to the public's great relief!

U

A United team at Wembley were due to play that day,
And it was urgent that an umpire should be found.
A unicorn from Uruguay, who'd returned to the U.K.
Said he understood the rules and knew the ground.

He felt it was uncanny that the weather wasn't calm,
For the wind was blowing up before the rain.
He was unduly anxious and he knew this caused him harm,
For his stomach ulcer gave unpleasant pain.

"I'll take my ukulele, and as usual when I fret,
I can strum upon it while the game's in play.
The team will be unanimous I shouldn't be upset,
And all the horrid wind and rain must go away."

He unearthed his red umbrella and a useful umber mack,
As he wanted to be dry upon the pitch,
And with ultrasonic whistle and a handy sandwich pack,
He urged the match to start without a hitch.

So in his umpire's uniform of ultramarine and white,
He gave the ultimatum that they start.
His whistle, from the U.S.A. was blown with all his might,
The game began, and he was doing his part.

But the match became an uproar, and playing became a feat,
And the wind became an ugly rushing sound.
The management were huddled on their soaked upholstered seats,
And wished that they were safely underground!

The goal posts were uprooted and caught them unawares,
The grass turned white and slippery with hail.
The terraces were emptied, people hurried down the stairs,
And the unicorn felt useless in the gale.

No one heard his utters, and nobody his sighs!
No one heard him calling out aloud!
He and his umbrella were wafted to the skies,
And were lost from sight in undulating cloud!

Most unicorns were umpires and have disappeared this way,
When unfortunately, weather's been so bad.
It's why they aren't seen anywhere and aren't around today,
And why the conservationists are sad!

V

A viper named Veronica was a vital, virile snake,
And was at variance with her diet, a vast and bad mistake.

With her voracious appetite – she liked venison and veal,
Though a vol-au-vent of vole and vetch had visual appeal.

With vigilance and vigour she'd catch victims with great
ease,
And after swallowing them whole, would vomit if you
please!

Then vertigo attacked her through a virus vile and rare.
She felt so very vulnerable with no one there to care.

It made her feel vindictive, quite violent, full of vice!
Her vivaciousness and charm had gone! She wasn't very
nice!

Her mood changed with a vengeance, her virtues vanished
fast,
Using venom with velocity that left her friends aghast!

Valiantly she found a vet while on the verge of tears.
He vaccinated her and vowed that she'd be fit for years!

And under a veranda with good views and ventilation,
She vegetated for a while, deciding her vocation.

She vacillated endlessly in a vacuum of self-doubt,
Visualising vaguely what life was all about.

She'd be an artist like Van Dyke and slosh on paint and
varnish,
But might end up a vagrant with reputation tarnished!

She could play on the viola, violin and double base,
And could recite some verse quite volubly with a fair
amount of grace.

But suddenly her vocal chords vibrated, not from choice,
And with such versatility, she could throw a varied voice!

So Veronica became a ventriloquist sublime,
Vindicating valuable talent every time.

The viper was so vibrant, she became a V.I.P.
You must visit her performance if in the vicinity!

W

Walter the worm, had met his Waterloo!
He'd got washed out from his wigwam in the wet.
He'd wiggle-waggled half the night to find a warmer home,
And was worried that he hadn't found one yet.

His waterproof watch was working, but his wallet had been
lost.
He wished he'd got a walkie-talkie set.
But then got welcomed by a weevil to a warehouse which
was warm,
It was wonderful! The best that he could get!

They sat upon two wicker chairs, with whiskey and with
wine,
And whispered to each other for a while.
Although the worm felt wanted, he was whimsical and sad
That the weevil's wit was warped and not his style!

And after words on Wall Street, the Stock Exchange and
wealth,
The worm felt well, not weary, weak or worn,
So left the warmth and comfort, made his way across the
floor,
And wobbled through a window to the dawn.

Whistling quite winsomely with a weird and warbling sound,
He wisely thought that he should have a wife.
He'd find one willy-nilly, some wayward, happy wench
Who'd play whist with him, and settle down for life.

And wandering along he heard a whimper, wail and whine,
A wheel had squashed a girl worm in the dirt.
It hadn't missed her by a whisker but had cut her waist in two!
Walter bound the bits together with his shirt!

He wound the cloth quite gently, and wrapped the wound up tight,
Wreathed his body close, and wooed her not to weep.
The warp and weft of the material, and the softness of the weave
Helped the wretched girl relax and get some sleep.

They entered wedlock happily on Wednesday that week,
At a wedding with some worms from far and wide.
He'd waited for this moment, it was a whim he had fulfilled,
And all in white, she made a willing, worthy bride!

Their honeymoon was spent in a wherry in the wind,
Where they whisked and whirled and waltzed in wildest joy.
The weather worsened slightly but their world was snug and whole,
They wound down the sail and anchored to a buoy.

They wondered whether they should leave, so waded to a bank,
Through waterweed and past a field of wheat.
And in a nearby warren found a homestead going to waste
Where they'd all that they could want amongst the peat.

He became a waiter with a worthwhile weekly wage,
Though weakly winked at widows when he could!
But served his walnut waffles with wafers and ice-cream,
And with wisdom ceased to waiver, which was good!

She became a wizard at whatever craft she tried,
Whittling willow wood with whetted knife,

And making wedge shaped candles with wadding, wax and wick,
So the happy worms were quite set up for life!

So when you go out walking, on the moor or in the woods,
Or along the lanes with grass at either edge.
If you see Walter or his wife in a place they shouldn't be,
Whip them up, and kindly put them in the hedge!

X

It's very hard to find a word that starts with 'X'!
It's often at the end, as in a word like 'vex'.
If you take a word like 'axe', then 'X' comes in the middle.
But words that start with 'X' sound like a sort of riddle!
Xenolith and xiphoid, and of course there's xylograph,
But trying to pronounce them is enough to make you laugh!
Xeropohilous – you can adapt to land extremely dry,
Or you could have xerophthalmia – inflammation of the eye.
Xanthain Marbles, are sculptures of long ago I'm told.
And xanthophyll's the colouring of leaves that turn to gold.
A xebec is an ancient craft, three masted, sailed by men,
And 'X' in Roman numerals, as a symbol, stands for '10'.
Xmas – that means Christmas, but it's not a proper word.
It's a funny sort of letter, and doesn't spell as it is heard!
For it's very often happiest when started with an 'E',
Like 'exactly' and 'explosion' and 'exercise' you see.
Of course there are the X-rays that photograph each bone,
But in algebra, the quantity of 'X' is quite unknown!
I'm sure you're good at sending a text and using Fax
And get furious as we all do, when sorting out your tax!
A xylophone's an instrument with bars from big to small,
But it's sounded with an 'S' again, and not an 'X' at all!
So it's very hard to find a word that starts with 'X'!
It's often at the end, as in a word like 'vex'.

Y

Now at the Tower of London, a Yeoman of the Guard
Had made a strange acquaintance with a yak.
But at Yule time, on Christmas Day, he found it very hard,
For Her Majesty had given him the sack!
"You cannot keep an animal," Her Majesty explained,
"You know that only ravens are allowed.
Year in, year out, the tourists come, the birds for this are trained.
Your yak would only panic in a crowd!"
And the Yeoman groomed his yak,
Collecting hair within a sack.

So with his hard-earned savings, the Yeoman bought a yacht,
A Yale design, it was a Yankee boat!
The yak was good at sailing, and knew every seaman's knot,
And so they had a yearn to be afloat.
And with a 'Yo-heave-ho!' they left from Traitor's Gate,
And yodelled as they caught the evening tide.
They had some fish for supper as they'd got a yam for bait,
And felt so young and happy with the ride.
And the Yeoman groomed his yak,
Collecting hair within a sack.

They set their yellow sails and their friendship grew quite fast,
They sometimes read from Browning, Keats or Yeats.
They told each other yarns as they sailed before the mast,
Reaching Yarmouth as inseparable mates.
Next they joined the Y.H.A. and hitch-hiked up to York,
And would not yield to sleepiness or yawns,

They saw the famous Minster, and bought yoghurt, yeast and pork,
And travelled back to Norfolk eating prawns.
And the Yeoman groomed his yak,
Collecting hair within a sack.

The Y.M.C.A. put them up, (its yew trees were a sight!)
With a yolk and brandy drink without delay.
They did their Yoga exercise by early morning light,
And returned to port to take their yacht away.
Yesterday, I heard that the Yeoman's spun a coat
From the long and silken hairs within the sack.
They now look so alike that if you see them on their boat,
It's hard to tell the Yeoman from the yak!
And the Yeoman groomed his yak,
Collecting hair within a sack.

Z

Zachariah was a zebra, and Zedekiah too,
And with their brother Zebedee, were triplets at the zoo.
At first they'd lived in Zanzibar, the place where they were
born,
And knew a zany rhino with a very twisty horn.
But he talked of education and the countries they should see.
They thought they'd try New Zealand, or perhaps the Zuider
Zee.
And after much discussion, and with their usual zeal,
They came to the conclusion that Zurich had appeal.
Their Zodiac sign was good, a departure date was set.
"We'll travel there by Zeppelin, and not by Jumbo jet."
They'd glance at the Zambezi and have a look at Crete,
And felt they didn't want to zoom to thirty thousand feet!
They'd rather zig-zag gently, and float above the ground,
And drift past all the mineshafts where tin and zinc were
found.

So soon the three got airborne, through the night and through
the day,
Sometimes playing their zither to pass the time away.
And when they got to Switzerland, and Zurich had been
found,
With instruments at zero, they landed on the ground.
And at the University they studied with such zest,
Attending each tutorial without a pause for rest.
First they did zoology to get a good degree,
Then zoography to learn the distribution of the flea!
They bulged with all their knowledge, and their skins got far
too tight!
They got so fat with learning that they really were a sight!

And getting their diploma, and feeling very proud,
They realised they would burst apart in front of all the crowd!
Then Zebedee awoke, not knowing what to do,
But all was just a dream! He'd been sleeping in the zoo!